French Word of the Day:

365 High Frequency Words to Accelerate Your French Vocabulary

Copyright © 2016

All rights reserved. No part of this publication may be reproduced, distributed, or transmitted in any form or by any means, including photocopying, recording, or other electronic or mechanical methods, without the prior written permission of the publisher.

Cover image by Jason Geurts

ISBN: 1534998543
ISBN-13: 978-1534998544

CONTENTS

Introduction	i
January	1
February	9
March	16
April	24
May	32
June	40
July	48
August	56
September	64
October	72
November	80
December	88

INTRODUCTION

Learning a new language involves learning a lot of new vocabulary. Although the grammar and pronunciation of a language can seem like the most difficult parts, especially a difficult language like French, the real challenge quickly becomes learning the thousands of new words you require to speak a new language fluently.

How to find the right words and how to efficiently memorize them are the problems that many language learners face near the beginning of their studies. The goal of this book is to fill the gap by providing you with a new, high frequency French word to learn every day. At the end of the year (or much sooner) you will be 365 words closer to your goal of speaking French.

Did you know that in English, the most common 100 words make up nearly half of every sentence, and that other languages have similar frequency distributions? This is a powerful concept that is underused in many language courses. By focusing on the high frequency words, this book will accelerate your French vocabulary more efficiently than merely learning the random lists of words that learners sometimes face, and by providing the words to you, this book will save you from the time-consuming process of searching for all those new words yourself.

The outline of this book is a new word every day for a year. In this way you can be sure that you are making progress even on days where you don't have time to study. Carry this word around with you and review it throughout

INTRODUCTION

the day. Of course many people will progress faster through this book and will want more than one word a day and in that case the reader should go at whatever pace feels comfortable. I would still encourage you go back to the word of the day to review on that specific day, just to ensure that you have thoroughly learned it. Remember repetition is the mother of all learning.

Good luck on your language learning journey and I hope you enjoy your French Word of the Day!

FRENCH WORD OF THE DAY

FRENCH ALPHABET AND PRONUNCIATION

The French language uses the same Latin alphabet as English, with the addition of some vowel accents. Most French letters are pronounced in a similar way to English, with some important exceptions.

French can be a difficult language to pronounce for an English speaker. There are many silent letters (especially at the end of a word) and some sounds that do not exist in English. However, there is a definite pattern to pronouncing French and once you are exposed to the language it becomes a lot easier. If you are unsure about the pronunciation, I recommend going to forvo.com and typing in the French word to hear a native speaker pronounce it.

There are two noun genders in French - masculine and feminine. The gender of the noun is important to know, as the noun and adjective forms are affected by the noun's gender. The gender is given below each noun in this book so that it can be learned along with the word on that day.

FRENCH WORD OF THE DAY

Jan. 1

couper

to cut

Jan. 2

pierre

stone (feminine)

Jan. 3

sac

bag (masculine)

Jan. 4

soupe

soup (feminine)

JANUARY

Jan. 5

triste

sad

Jan. 6

hiver

winter (masculine)

Jan. 7

grimper

to climb

Jan. 8

arbe

tree (masculine)

FRENCH WORD OF THE DAY

Jan. 9

lire

to read

Jan. 10

assiette

plate (feminine)

Jan. 11

tante

aunt (feminine)

Jan. 12

neige

snow (feminine)

Jan. 13

avocat

lawyer (masculine)

Jan. 14

robe

dress (feminine)

Jan. 15

qui

who

Jan. 16

riche

rich

FRENCH WORD OF THE DAY

Jan. 17

bateau

boat (masculine)

Jan. 18

manger

to eat

Jan. 19

garer

to park

Jan. 20

eau

water (feminine)

Jan. 21

train

train (masculine)

Jan. 22

cher

expensive

Jan. 23

toujours

always

Jan. 24

déjà

already

FRENCH WORD OF THE DAY

Jan. 25

paix

peace (feminine)

Jan. 26

soldat

soldier (masculine)

Jan. 27

tuer

to kill

Jan. 28

sentir

to smell

JANUARY

Jan. 29

journal

newspaper (masculine)

Jan. 30

visage

face (feminine)

Jan. 31

ferme

farm (feminine)

FRENCH WORD OF THE DAY

Feb. 1

famille

family (feminine)

Feb. 2

grand

big

Feb. 3

jeter

to throw

Feb. 4

court

short

Feb. 5

corps

body (masculine)

Feb. 6

lent

slow

Feb. 7

peut-être

maybe

Feb. 8

portefeuille

wallet (masculine)

FRENCH WORD OF THE DAY

Feb. 9

danser

to dance

Feb. 10

papier

paper (masculine)

Feb. 11

nez

nose (masculine)

Feb. 12

sueur

sweat (feminine)

Feb. 13

se rappeler

to remember

Feb. 14

sec

dry

Feb. 15

téléviseur

television (masculine)

Feb. 16

jambe

leg (feminine)

FRENCH WORD OF THE DAY

Feb. 17

cerveau

brain (masculine)

Feb. 18

épais

thick

Feb. 19

attraper

to catch

Feb. 20

bol

bowl (masculine)

FEBRUARY

Feb. 21

ciel

sky (masculine)

Feb. 22

fameux

famous

Feb. 23

monde

world (masculine)

Feb. 24

appartement

apartment (masculine)

FRENCH WORD OF THE DAY

Feb. 25

jour

day (masculine)

Feb. 26

jaune

yellow

Feb. 27

vêtements

clothing (masculine)

Feb. 28

fleuve

river (masculine)

MARCH

Mar. 1

chien

dog (masculine)

Mar. 2

voler

to fly

Mar. 3

se réveiller

to wake up

Mar. 4

minute

minute (feminine)

FRENCH WORD OF THE DAY

Mar. 5

sauter

to jump

Mar. 6

an

year (masculine)

Mar. 7

tasse

cup (feminine)

Mar. 8

air

air (masculine)

Mar. 9

vache

cow (feminine)

Mar. 10

police

police (feminine)

Mar. 11

quoi

what

Mar. 12

semaine

week (feminine)

FRENCH WORD OF THE DAY

Mar. 13

embrasser

to kiss

Mar. 14

poche

pocket (feminine)

Mar. 15

vélo

bicycle (masculine)

Mar. 16

comment

how

Mar. 17

noir

black

Mar. 18

langue

language (feminine)

Mar. 19

jeu

game (masculine)

Mar. 20

poivre

pepper (masculine)

FRENCH WORD OF THE DAY

Mar. 21

grand-mère

grandmother (feminine)

Mar. 22

toilettes

bathroom / toilet (plural)

Mar. 23

être assis

to sit

Mar. 24

cheveux

hair (masculine)

Mar. 25

belle

beautiful

Mar. 26

science

science (feminine)

Mar. 27

carte

map (feminine)

Mar. 28

lit

bed (masculine)

FRENCH WORD OF THE DAY

Mar. 29

bureau

desk (masculine)

Mar. 30

poisson

fish (masculine)

Mar. 31

appareil photo

camera (masculine)

Apr. 1

tirer

to pull

Apr. 2

automne

autumn (masculine)

Apr. 3

écouter

to listen

Apr. 4

musée

museum (masculine)

FRENCH WORD OF THE DAY

Apr. 5

différent

different

Apr. 6

nouveau

new

Apr. 7

voiture

car (feminine)

Apr. 8

même

same

APRIL

Apr. 9

humain

human (masculine)

Apr. 10

écrire

to write

Apr. 11

chat

cat (masculine)

Apr. 12

clé

key (feminine)

FRENCH WORD OF THE DAY

Apr. 13

musique

music (feminine)

Apr. 14

travailler

to work

Apr. 15

orange

orange (color)

Apr. 16

pneu

tire (masculine)

Apr. 17

herbe

grass (feminine)

Apr. 18

quelqu'un

somebody

Apr. 19

végétarien

vegetarian

Apr. 20

fort

strong

FRENCH WORD OF THE DAY

Apr. 21

vouloir

to want

Apr. 22

village

village (masculine)

Apr. 23

nord

north (masculine)

Apr. 24

jambon

ham (masculine)

Apr. 25

ordinateur

computer (masculine)

Apr. 26

droite

right (side) (feminine)

Apr. 27

tard

late

Apr. 28

nuit

night (feminine)

FRENCH WORD OF THE DAY

Apr. 29

bouche

mouth (feminine)

Apr. 30

bras

arm (masculine)

MAY

May 1

rien

nothing

May 2

quand

when

May 3

beaucoup

many

May 4

fort

loud

FRENCH WORD OF THE DAY

May 5

garçon

boy (masculine)

May 6

idée

idea (feminine)

May 7

problème

problem (masculine)

May 8

gare

train station (feminine)

May 9

banane

banana (feminine)

May 10

blanc

white

May 11

cuisine

kitchen (feminine)

May 12

ouvrir

to open

FRENCH WORD OF THE DAY

May 13

pays

country (masculine)

May 14

thé

tea (masculine)

May 15

pomme de terre

potato (feminine)

May 16

sud

south (masculine)

May 17

chanter

to sing

May 18

heureux

happy

May 19

fille

daughter (feminine)

May 20

cou

neck (masculine)

FRENCH WORD OF THE DAY

May 21

finir

to end

May 22

marcher

to walk

May 23

art

art (masculine)

May 24

cuisiner

to cook

May 25

petit déjeuner

breakfast (masculine)

May 26

homme

man (masculine)

May 27

école

school (feminine)

May 28

sale

dirty

FRENCH WORD OF THE DAY

May 29

plastique

plastic (masculine)

May 30

glace

ice (feminine)

May 31

cheval

horse (masculine)

Jun. 1

heure

hour (feminine)

Jun. 2

lumière

light (feminine)

Jun. 3

rouge

red

Jun. 4

crayon

pencil (masculine)

FRENCH WORD OF THE DAY

Jun. 5

en vie

alive

Jun. 6

père

father (masculine)

Jun. 7

livre

book (masculine)

Jun. 8

mouillé

wet

Jun. 9

fruit

fruit (masculine)

Jun. 10

oublier

to forget

Jun. 11

rêve

dream (masculine)

Jun. 12

pauvre

poor

FRENCH WORD OF THE DAY

Jun. 13

langue

tongue (feminine)

Jun. 14

bon marché

cheap

Jun. 15

mer

sea (feminine)

Jun. 16

suivre

to follow

Jun. 17

soleil

sun (masculine)

Jun. 18

printemps

spring (season) (masculine)

Jun. 19

pont

bridge (masculine)

Jun. 20

mentir

to tell a lie

FRENCH WORD OF THE DAY

Jun. 21

trouver

to find

Jun. 22

où

where

Jun. 23

pain

bread (masculine)

Jun. 24

pousser

to push

Jun. 25

hier

yesterday

Jun. 26

commencer

to begin

Jun. 27

intelligent

intelligent

Jun. 28

froid

cold

Jun. 29

beurre

butter (masculine)

Jun. 30

salle de classe

classroom (feminine)

JULY

Jul. 1

regarder

to look

Jul. 2

penser

to think

Jul. 3

laver

to wash

Jul. 4

café

coffee (masculine)

FRENCH WORD OF THE DAY

Jul. 5

restaurant

restaurant (masculine)

Jul. 6

légume

vegetable (masculine)

Jul. 7

pièce

room (feminine)

Jul. 8

chaud

hot

Jul. 9

bœuf

beef (masculine)

Jul. 10

billet

ticket (masculine)

Jul. 11

bébé

baby (masculine)

Jul. 12

rire

to laugh

FRENCH WORD OF THE DAY

Jul. 13

glace

ice cream (feminine)

Jul. 14

avenir

future (masculine)

Jul. 15

oreille

ear (feminine)

Jul. 16

médicament

medicine (masculine)

Jul. 17

parc

park (masculine)

Jul. 18

voix

voice (feminine)

Jul. 19

dormir

to sleep

Jul. 20

étoile

star (feminine)

FRENCH WORD OF THE DAY

Jul. 21

silencieux

quiet

Jul. 22

oncle

uncle (masculine)

Jul. 23

forêt

forest (feminine)

Jul. 24

tomate

tomato (feminine)

Jul. 25

lèvre

lip (feminine)

Jul. 26

boire

to drink

Jul. 27

propre

clean

Jul. 28

parler

to speak

FRENCH WORD OF THE DAY

Jul. 29

dos

back (body) (masculine)

Jul. 30

lac

lake (masculine)

Jul. 31

souris

mouse (masculine)

AUGUST

Aug. 1

acheter

to buy

Aug. 2

frapper

to hit

Aug. 3

peau

skin (feminine)

Aug. 4

cœur

heart (masculine)

FRENCH WORD OF THE DAY

Aug. 5

fille

girl (feminine)

Aug. 6

vent

wind (masculine)

Aug. 7

pistolet

gun (masculine)

Aug. 8

moins

less

AUGUST

Aug. 9

culture

culture (feminine)

Aug. 10

pomme

apple (feminine)

Aug. 11

aujourd'hui

today

Aug. 12

gagner

to win

FRENCH WORD OF THE DAY

Aug. 13

sourire

to smile

Aug. 14

mince

thin

Aug. 15

orange

orange (fruit) (feminine)

Aug. 16

épouse

wife (feminine)

Aug. 17

demain

tomorrow

Aug. 18

été

summer (masculine)

Aug. 19

ville

city (feminine)

Aug. 20

fils

son (masculine)

FRENCH WORD OF THE DAY

Aug. 21

aider

to help

Aug. 22

mort

dead

Aug. 23

bureau

office (masculine)

Aug. 24

grandir

to grow

Aug. 25

pantalon

pants (masculine)

Aug. 26

mois

month (masculine)

Aug. 27

cochon

pig (masculine)

Aug. 28

quelque chose

something

FRENCH WORD OF THE DAY

Aug. 29

feuille

leaf (feminine)

Aug. 30

malade

sick / ill

Aug. 31

fermer

to close

Sep. 1

loup

wolf (masculine)

Sep. 2

feu

fire (masculine)

Sep. 3

bière

beer (feminine)

Sep. 4

table

table (feminine)

Sep. 5

vin

wine (masculine)

Sep. 6

cerise

cherry (feminine)

Sep. 7

se battre

to fight

Sep. 8

payer

to pay

Sep. 9

nager

to swim

Sep. 10

sel

salt (masculine)

Sep. 11

perdre

to lose (game etc.)

Sep. 12

réunion

meeting (feminine)

FRENCH WORD OF THE DAY

Sep. 13

costume

suit (masculine)

Sep. 14

travail

job (masculine)

Sep. 15

œuf

egg (masculine)

Sep. 16

rue

street (feminine)

Sep. 17

oiseau

bird (masculine)

Sep. 18

aimer

to love

Sep. 19

sport

sport (masculine)

Sep. 20

difficile

difficult

Sep. 21

rapidement

fast / quickly

Sep. 22

matin

morning (masculine)

Sep. 23

salade

salad (feminine)

Sep. 24

mur

wall (masculine)

SEPTEMBER

Sep. 25

courir

to run

Sep. 26

pluie

rain (feminine)

Sep. 27

jardin

garden (masculine)

Sep. 28

tomber

to fall

FRENCH WORD OF THE DAY

Sep. 29

mourir

to die

Sep. 30

poulet

chicken (masculine)

Oct. 1

étroit

narrow

Oct. 2

médecin

doctor (masculine)

Oct. 3

orteil

toe (masculine)

Oct. 4

tôt

early

FRENCH WORD OF THE DAY

Oct. 5

horloge

clock (feminine)

Oct. 6

chaise

chair (feminine)

Oct. 7

jus

juice (masculine)

Oct. 8

pleurer

to cry

Oct. 9

carotte

carrot (feminine)

Oct. 10

étudiant

student (masculine)

Oct. 11

sang

blood (masculine)

Oct. 12

apprendre

to learn

FRENCH WORD OF THE DAY

Oct. 13

laid

ugly

Oct. 14

doigt

finger (masculine)

Oct. 15

long

long

Oct. 16

avion

airplane (masculine)

Oct. 17

voir

to see

Oct. 18

huile

oil (cooking) (feminine)

Oct. 19

autobus

bus (masculine)

Oct. 20

petit

small

FRENCH WORD OF THE DAY

Oct. 21

savoir

to know

Oct. 22

mère

mother (feminine)

Oct. 23

espérer

to hope

Oct. 24

aéroport

airport (masculine)

Oct. 25

important

important

Oct. 26

tête

head (feminine)

Oct. 27

argent

money (masculine)

Oct. 28

facile

easy

Oct. 29

mariage

wedding (masculine)

Oct. 30

montagne

mountain (feminine)

Oct. 31

agneau

lamb (masculine)

NOVEMBER

Nov. 1

île

island (feminine)

Nov. 2

haut

tall

Nov. 3

ami

friend (masculine)

Nov. 4

nom

name (masculine)

FRENCH WORD OF THE DAY

Nov. 5

histoire

history (feminine)

Nov. 6

raisin

grape (masculine)

Nov. 7

chapeau

hat (masculine)

Nov. 8

chaussette

sock (feminine)

NOVEMBER

Nov. 9

bar

bar (place to drink) (masculine)

Nov. 10

enseignant

teacher (masculine)

Nov. 11

ours

bear (masculine)

Nov. 12

faible

weak

Nov. 13

faire

to make

Nov. 14

déjeuner

lunch (masculine)

Nov. 15

ennuyeux

boring

Nov. 16

barbe

beard (feminine)

Nov. 17

construire

to build

Nov. 18

bleu

blue

Nov. 19

botte

boot (feminine)

Nov. 20

grand-père

grandfather (masculine)

FRENCH WORD OF THE DAY

Nov. 21

œil

eye (masculine)

Nov. 22

chambre

bedroom (feminine)

Nov. 23

personne

nobody

Nov. 24

porte

door (feminine)

NOVEMBER

Nov. 25

frère

brother (masculine)

Nov. 26

lune

moon (feminine)

Nov. 27

dent

tooth (feminine)

Nov. 28

cuillère

spoon (feminine)

FRENCH WORD OF THE DAY

Nov. 29

manteau

coat (masculine)

Nov. 30

large

wide

DECEMBER

Dec. 1

ouest

west (masculine)

Dec. 2

stylo

pen (masculine)

Dec. 3

parapluie

umbrella (masculine)

Dec. 4

gauche

left (feminine)

FRENCH WORD OF THE DAY

Dec. 5

moitié

half (feminine)

Dec. 6

dîner

dinner (masculine)

Dec. 7

époux

husband (masculine)

Dec. 8

vendre

to sell

Dec. 9

arme

weapon (feminine)

Dec. 10

gâteau

cake (masculine)

Dec. 11

fromage

cheese (masculine)

Dec. 12

sœur

sister (feminine)

FRENCH WORD OF THE DAY

Dec. 13

maintenant

now

Dec. 14

conduire

to drive

Dec. 15

femme

woman (feminine)

Dec. 16

guerre

war (feminine)

Dec. 17

métal

metal (masculine)

Dec. 18

hôpital

hospital (masculine)

Dec. 19

lait

milk (masculine)

Dec. 20

maison

house (feminine)

FRENCH WORD OF THE DAY

Dec. 21

vert

green

Dec. 22

chaussure

shoe (feminine)

Dec. 23

hôtel

hotel (masculine)

Dec. 24

magasin

store / shop (masculine)

Dec. 25

intéressant

interesting

Dec. 26

est

east (masculine)

Dec. 27

jouer

to play

Dec. 28

église

church (feminine)

FRENCH WORD OF THE DAY

Dec. 29

jupe

skirt (feminine)

Dec. 30

pile

battery (feminine)

Dec. 31

fleur

flower (feminine)

Made in the USA
Las Vegas, NV
08 October 2023